Ideology and the Child

PETER HOLLINE

IDEOLOGY.4. A systematic scheme of ideas, or society, or to the conduct of a class or group, and regarded as justifying actions, esp. one that is held implicitly or adopted as a whole and maintained regardless of the course of events.

—Oxford English Dictionary

I will start with an assortment of disconnected statements.

It is a good thing for children to read fiction.

Children's own tastes are important.

Some novels for children are better than others.

It is a good thing to help children to enjoy better books than they did before.

A good children's book is not necessarily more difficult or less enjoyable than a bad children's book.

Children are individuals, and have different tastes.

Children of different ages tend to like different sorts of books.

Children of different ethnic and social backgrounds may differ in their tastes and needs.

Some books written for children are liked by adults.

Some books written for adults are liked by children.

Adults and children may like (or dislike) the same book for different reasons.

Children are influenced by what they read.

Adults are influenced by what they read.

A novel written for children may be a good novel even if children in general do not enjoy it.

A novel written for children may be a bad novel even if children in general do enjoy it.

Every story is potentially influential for all its readers.

A novel may be influential in ways that its author did not anticipate or intend.

All novels embody a set of values, whether intentionally or not.

A book may be well written yet embody values that in a particular society are widely deplored.

A book may be badly written yet embody values that in a particular society are widely approved.

3

A book may be undesirable for children because of the values it embodies.

The same book may mean different things to different children.

It is sensible to pay attention to children's judgement of books, whether or not most adults share them.

It is sensible to pay attention to adults' judgements of children's books, whether or not most children share them.

Some of these statements are clearly paired or linked, but they can be read separately in isolation. All of them seem to me to be truisms. It would surprise me if any serious commentator on children's reading were to quarrel seriously with any of them. He or she might wish to qualify them, to respond as to Dr F.R. Leavis's famous 'This is so, isn't it?' with his permitted answer, 'Yes, but . . .'. Even so, I would expect a very wide consensus.

However, if this series of statements is brought to bear on the controversy in recent years between so-called book people and so-called child people, it will be found I think that most of them drift naturally towards either one side or the other. In particular, there is likely to be a somewhat one-sided emphasis on remarks about adult judgements and their importance (book people); about children's judgements and their importance (child people); about differences of literary merit (book people) and about the influence on readers of a book's social and political values (child people).

If these two little exercises do indeed produce the results that I expect them to, much of the division between literary and social priorities which has arisen over the last fifteen years or so may come to seem exaggerated and sterile. We have differences of emphasis disguised as differences of principle. (This may have happened because the extremes of each alternative reflect a much larger public controversy about the chief purpose of education. People slip without realizing it from talking about children's books to talking about educational philosophy.) One result is particularly odd. By my own idiosyncratic but convinced reckoning, the statements which are left over, which seem not to bend towards the critical priorities of either side, are those which concern the individuality of children, and differences of taste or need between children and adults or between one child or group of children and another. It is a curious fact that these, the most obvious truisms of all, are also the most contentious statements. They are contentious because on the one hand they cast doubt on the supremacy of adult literary judgement, and on the other they suggest that we cannot generalize about children's interests.

4

It is very easy and tempting to simplify a debate until its nature becomes conveniently binary, and matters which are not associated by any kind of logical necessity, or even loosely connected, become coalesced in the same ideological system. Something of this sort has happened in the schism between child people and book people. In the evolution of debate, the child people have become associated not only with a prime concern with the child reader rather than the literary artefact but with the propagation through children's books of a 'progressive' ideology expressed through social values. The book people, on the other hand, have become linked with a broadly conservative and 'reactionary' ideological position. The result is a crude but damaging conjunction of attitudes on each side, not as it necessarily is but as it is perceived by the other. A concern for the literary quality of children's books as works of imagination has become linked in a caricatured manifesto with indifference to the child reader and with tolerance or approval of obsolete, or traditional, or 'reactionary' political values. A concern with the child reader has become linked with indifference to high standards of literary achievement and with populist ardour on behalf of the three political missions which are seen as most urgent in contemporary society: anti-racism, anti-sexism, and anti-classism.

If this is the general divide between book people and child people amongst the critics, a matching divide is said to exist between writers. The book people amongst authors – those who are said by hostile commentators to have produced the prize-winning, dust-collecting, adult-praised, child-neglected masterpieces of the illusory 'golden age' – are those who write 'to please themselves', or 'for the child I once was', or, in C.S. Lewis's famous remark, 'because a children's story is the best art-form for something you have to say.'[1] The child people amongst authors, on the other hand, would accept Robert Leeson's analogy between the modern author and the oral storyteller of days before the printed book:

> . . . is the public, the consumer, obliged to accept such a take-it-or-leave-it attitude, being grateful if the artistic arrows shot in the air find their target? What happened in the old story-telling days? If the audience did not appreciate the genius of the storyteller, did that individual stalk off, supperless, into the night? Actual experience of story-telling suggests something different. You match story to audience, as far as you can.[2]

The trouble with this packaging of attitudes is that it oversimplifies, trivializes and restricts the boundaries of debate. Admittedly most writers on both sides of the notional divide have at times unwisely offered hostages to fortune. One may take for instance Fred Inglis's remark:

> Irrespective of what the child makes of an experience, the adult wants to judge it for himself, and so doing means judging it for *itself*. This judgement comes first, and it is at least logically separable from doing the reckoning for children. *Tom's Midnight Garden* and *Puck of Pook's Hill* are wonderful books, whether or not your child can make head or tail of them.[3]

This carefully formulated and entirely sensible statement offers an important distinction between equally valid but separate ways of reviewing literary experience. Yet I have seen the last sentence removed from its context and made to seem like a wanton dismissal of the child, a typical instance of the book person's negligent aesthetics.

On the other side of the chasm is Bob Dixon, who follows an assault on ancient symbolic and metaphorical uses of the word 'black' by a paragraph which seems ready on ideological grounds to consign Shakespeare and Dickens to the incinerator:

> Adult literature, as might be expected, is full of such figurative and symbolic usages – when it isn't openly racist. Shylock and Fagin, Othello and Caliban all deserve a second look, for there's no need for anyone to accept racism in literature, not even if expressed in deathless blank verse.[4]

This is quite true. Any individual is free to elevate political judgement above literary judgement, and to be contemptuous of all literature which offends a political criterion. The converse is also true. Any individual is free to like and admire a great work of literature, even if its ideology is repellent. These are the private freedoms of a democratic society, and I hope that any commentator would defend both with equal enthusiasm. I make the second choice myself in the case of D.H. Lawrence, whom I admire as a great writer and whose ideology I detest. Neither principle is much use when we confront the problem of introducing children to great works of the past which do not entirely accord with current moral priorities. But if anyone says, 'We should not introduce them; we should ban them,' I begin to hear the boots of Nazis faintly treading, no matter what colour their uniforms.

My particular concern in this article is to argue that, in the very period when developments in literary theory have made us newly aware of the omnipresence of ideology in all literature, and the impossibility of confining its occurrence to visible surface features of a text, the study of ideology in children's literature has been increasingly restricted to such surface features by the polarities of critical debate. A desire on the part of the child people for a particular set of social outcomes has led to pressure for a literature to fit them, and a simplistic view of the manner in which a book's ideology is carried. In turn, this inevitably leads to a situation where too much stress is placed on *what* children read and too little on *how* they read it. At the very point in history when education seemed ready to accept the reading of fiction as a complex, important, but teachable skill, the extremities of critical opinion have devalued the element of skill in favour of the mere external substance.

Diversity and individuality

Things can be made to sound very easy, as they do in Robert Leeson's reassuring comments:

> This *is* a special literature. Its writers have special status in home and school, free to influence without direct responsibility for upbringing and care. This should not engender irresponsibility – on the contrary. It is very much a matter of respect, on the one hand for the fears and concerns of those who bring up and educate children, and on the other for the creative freedom of those whose lives are spent writing for them. I have generally found in discussion with parents or teachers, including those critical of or hostile to my work, that these respects are mutual.[5]

I should like to think that this was true and generally accepted. But it cannot, no matter how true, be so simple. In a socially and culturally, politically and racially divided country such as Britain (and most Western countries to some extent or other) there is not a uniform pattern of 'fears and concerns' on the part of 'those who bring up and educate children'. The 'fears and concerns' of a teacher in a preparatory school in Hampshire are likely to be substantially different from those of a primary school teacher in Liverpool; those of an Irish Catholic parent in Belfast will differ from those of an Asian parent in Bradford. I wish to make only the obvious but neglected point, that the same book, read by four children in the care of these four adults, will not in practice be the same book. It will be four different books. Each of these children needs and deserves a literature, but the literature which meets their needs is unlikely to be a homogeneous one.

It is of course important too for the writer's creative freedom to be respected. But in order to be respected it must be understood, and on that score also I do not share Robert Leeson's optimism. There is too much evidence of pressure on writers (from all points of the politico-moral spectrum) to conform to a predetermined ideology issuing in visible surface features of the text. Here, for example, is Nina Bawden, a writer widely admired by critics of very different approaches (see Fred Inglis, *The Promise of Happiness*, pages 267-70, and Robert Leeson, *Reading and Righting*, page 122):

> Speaking to people who care, often deeply, for children, I have begun to feel that the *child* I write for is mysteriously absent . . . 'Are you concerned, when you write, to see that girls are not forced into feminine role-playing?' 'What about the sexuality of children?' 'All writers are middle class, at least by the time they have become successful as writers, so what use are their books to working class/deprived/emotionally or educationally backward children?' 'Writers should write about modern (*sic*) problems, like drugs, schoolgirl pregnancies. Aren't the books you write rather escapist?' 'What do you know about the problems of the child in the high-rise flat since you have not lived in one?' To take this last question. The reply, that you project your imagination, is seldom taken as adequate; but what other one is there?[6]

Leeson's dictum, 'You match story to audience, as far as you can', is less straightforward than it seems. A diversity of authors exercising their 'creative freedom' – as they must, if they are to write anything worthwhile at all – will *only* match story to audience '*as far as they can*'. If there were indeed a single, uniform audience, a theoretical 'child' who stood for all children, there would be few problems. Either a writer would be able to match her story to this 'child', in which case her credentials as a children's writer would be proved, or she would not be able to, in which case she might have to settle for being a writer of those other children's books supposedly beloved of the book people, the ones admired by literary adults but unread by actual children.

However, one point I hoped to make with my opening anthology of truisms is that the most conspicuous truisms of all are ones which many adult commentators are in practice loth to accept. When Leeson says 'you match story to audience', he must surely be postulating many possible audiences, whether individual (parent reading to child) or socially grouped (teacher or visiting author reading to school class). It is clear that these audiences will differ greatly from each other, whether in age, or sex, or race, or social class, and that these different audiences will perceive the same story in different ways. Otherwise there would be no need for Robert Leeson to do any 'matching'. He is not suggesting that a writer who adjusts and improvises in order to make his story work with one group of children can then sit back, assured of its success with every other group thereafter. And yet at their own self-caricaturing extremes this is precisely the assumption on which both book people and child people seem to act.

For the caricatured book person (a *rara avis*, perhaps) the distinguished children's book has a quality of verbal imagination which can be shown to exist by adult interpretative analysis, and this is a transferable objective merit which the 'ideal' child reader (though unable of course to verbalize his experience) is capable of appreciating and enjoying. The good literary text has an external existence which transcends the difference between reader and reader, even between child and adult. Consequently there is an implicit definition of children's literature which has little *necessarily* to do with children: it is not the title of a readership but of a genre, collateral perhaps with fable or fantasy. Ideology will be admitted to have a place in it, but since the child audience and hence the teaching function are subordinate to literary and aesthetic considerations, it is a small part of the critic's responsibility to evaluate it.

For the caricatured child person the book exists chiefly in terms of audience response. The distinguished children's book is one which the 'kids' will like and which will aid their social growth. Historical periods will differ in the forms of social growth they cherish, but it is an article of faith that the current period will be wiser than its predecessors. The child audience, by some ideological sleight of hand, will be virtually identical or at the very least highly compatible with the preferred social objectives. In an age which desires to propagate imperialist sentiments, children will be an army of incipient colonizing pioneers. In an age which wishes to abolish differences between sexes, races and classes, the readership is a composite 'child' which is willing to be anti-sexist, anti-racist and anti-classist, and does not itself belong to any sex, or race, or class other than those which the equalizing literature is seeking to promote. The 'kids' are a Kid, who is sexless but female, colourless but black, classless but proletarian. Children's literature is implicitly defined as being for this Kid: it is not the title of a genre but of a readership.

Ideology is all-important to it. Literary merit will be admitted to have a place, but it is a minor part of the critic's responsibility to evaluate it.

Both these caricatures exist. Both are extremely intolerant of anything which lies outside their preferred agenda. The first kind is the one which says 'I am almost inclined to set it up as a canon that a children's story which is enjoyed only by children is a bad children's story.'[7] The second is the kind which says, as someone did of Robert Westall's brilliant anti-totalitarian story *Futuretrack 5*, 'The book will appeal greatly to teenage boys, which is the best reason for not buying it.' Both (though naturally for very different reasons) will abominate Enid Blyton, and perhaps it is true to say that both understand the effective working of ideology less well than she did, in practice if not in theory.

My purpose here is emphatically not to argue for or against any single ideological structure in children's books (and certainly not to vindicate Miss Blyton's), but to contend that ideology is an inevitable, untameable and largely uncontrollable factor in the transaction between books and children, and that it is so because of the multiplicity and diversity of both 'book' and 'child' and of the social world in which each of these seductive abstractions takes a plenitude of individual forms. Our priority in the world of children's books should not be to promote ideology but to understand it, and find ways of helping others to understand it, including the children themselves.

Three levels of ideology

Ideology, then, is present in a children's book in three main ways. The first and most tractable is made up of the explicit social, political or moral beliefs of the individual writer, and his wish to recommend them to children through the story. An attractive example is this, offered by the late Henry Treece:

> I feel that children will come to no harm if, in their stories, an ultimate justice is shown to prevail, if, in spite of hard times, the characters come through to receive what they deserve. This, after all, is a hope which most of us share – that all may yet be well provided that we press on with courage and faith. So in my stories I try to tell the children that life may be difficult and unpredictable, and that even the most commendable characters may suffer injustice and misery for a while, but that the joy is in the doing, the effort, and that self-pity has no place. And at the end and the gods willing, the good man who holds to the permanent virtues of truthfulness, loyalty and a certain

10

sort of stoic acceptance both of life's pains and pleasures, will be the fulfilled man. If that is not true, then, for me, nothing is true: and this is what I try to tell the children.[8]

This is the most conspicuous element in the ideology of children's books, and the easiest to detect. Its presence is conscious, deliberate and in some measure 'pointed', even when as with Treece there is nothing unusual or unfamiliar in the message the writer is hoping to convey.

It is at this level of intended surface ideology that fiction carries new ideas, non-conformist or revolutionary attitudes, and efforts to change imaginative awareness in line with contemporary social criticism. This causes difficulties both for writers and critics, which can be exemplified from present-day concern with the depiction of sexual roles. There are hundreds of books which passively borrow and reproduce the sexual stereotyping which they inherit from earlier fiction. No one notices, except radical adult readers (and perhaps some children) who are alert to it and offended by it. On the other hand, any novel which questions the stereotypes and sets out to reflect anti-sexist attitudes will almost inevitably do so conspicuously because it depicts surprising rather than customary behaviour. Ironically, the astonishing effect of *The Turbulent Term of Tyke Tiler* as an anti-sexist story is largely due to its ingenious self-disguise. Much the same is true of anti-racist or anti-classist fiction. In so far as it diverges from stock assumptions about race or class, it may seem crudely didactic. If on the other hand the author seeks to present as natural a society without racial prejudice or class division and to leave out tutelary scenes of conflict, she risks blunting the ideological content and presenting happenings which readers simply do not believe. The writer faces a dilemma: it is very difficult in contemporary Britain to write an anti-sexist, anti-racist or anti-classist novel without revealing that these are still objectives, principles and ideals rather than the realities of predictable everyday behaviour. If you present as natural and commonplace the behaviour you would *like* to be natural and commonplace, you risk muting the social effectiveness of your story. If you dramatize the social tensions, you risk a superficial ideological stridency.

The writer may opt for more circuitous methods. The more gifted the writer, the more likely to do so. If the fictional world is fully imagined and realized, it may carry its ideological burden more covertly, showing things as they are but trusting to literary organization rather than explicitly didactic guidelines to achieve a moral effect. Misunderstandings may follow if you are unlucky or too trusting. The hand of anti-racist censorship has begun to fall occasionally on the greatest anti-racist text in all literature, *Huckleberry Finn*. Twain's ideological error is to be always supremely the novelist rather than the preacher, to present his felt truth uncompromisingly rather than opt for educative adjustments to it, and to trust the intelligence of his readers. Perhaps the most luminous moment in anti-racist storytelling comes when Huck, arriving at the Phelpses' farm and being mistaken for Tom Sawyer, has to fabricate an excuse for late arrival by inventing a river-boat mishap:

> 'It warn't the grounding – that didn't keep us back but a little. We blowed out a cylinder-head.'
>   'Good gracious! anybody hurt?'
>   'No'm. Killed a nigger.'
>   'Well, it's lucky; because sometimes people do get hurt . . . '[9]

This snatch of dialogue is a devastating sign of what comes naturally to Huck's mind as soon as he begins to role-play Tom, but its full effect depends on its late placing in the novel, in the wake of all we have seen already of Huck's 'sound heart and deformed conscience'. It is a crucial point: you cannot experience the book as an anti-racist text unless you know *how to read a novel*. In modern children's writing the consciously didactic text rarely displays such confidence in its readers, with the unhappy result that reformist ideological explicitness is often achieved at the cost of imaginative depth.

The inference is clear: in literature as in life the undeserved advantage lies with *passive* ideology. The second category of ideological content which we must thus take into account is the individual writer's unexamined assumptions. As soon as these are admitted to be relevant, it becomes impossible to confine ideology to a writer's conscious intentions or articulated messages, and necessary to accept that all children's literature is inescapably didactic:

> Since children's literature is didactic it must by definition be a repository, in a literate society almost the quintessential source, of the values that parents and others hope to teach to the next generation.[10]

This is merely to accept what is surely obvious: writers for children (like writers for adults) cannot hide what their values are. Even if beliefs are passive and unexamined, and no part of any conscious proselytising, the texture of language and story will reveal them and communicate them. The working of ideology at this level is not incidental or unimportant. It might seem that values whose presence can only be convincingly demonstrated by an adult with some training in critical skills are unlikely to carry much potency with children. More probably the reverse is true: the values at stake are usually those which are taken for granted by the writer, and reflect the writer's integration in a society which unthinkingly accepts them. In turn this means that children, unless they are helped to notice what is there, will take them for granted too. Unexamined, passive values are widely *shared* values, and we should not underestimate the powers of reinforcement vested in quiescent and unconscious ideology.

Again I will take a pleasant example. It occurs in Richmal Crompton's *William the Bad*. Henry is summing up the salient features of British party politics before the gang hold their elections:

> 'There's four sorts of people tryin' to get to be rulers. They all want to make things better, but they want to make 'em better in different ways. There's Conservatives, an' they want to make things better by keepin' 'em jus' like what they are now. An' there's Liberals, an' they want to make things better by alterin' them jus' a bit, but not so's anyone'd notice, an' there's Socialists, an' they want to make things better by takin' everyone's money off 'em an' there's Communists an' they want to make things better by killin' everyone but themselves.'[11]

This is fun, and not to be taken solemnly, but it is not exactly even-handed fun. I do not think Miss Crompton is deliberately making propaganda, but there is not much doubt where her own sympathies lie or where she tacitly assumes that the reader's will follow. The joke about Conservatives and Liberals is a joke about *our sort*, and the joke about Socialists and Communists is a joke about a *different sort*. The interest of the example lies in the gentle, unconsidered bias of the humour. Behind it lies an assumption of uncontroversial familiarity. It can be an instructive exercise to recast the joke, so that its bias dips in the opposite direction – suppose, for example, that it began its list with 'There's Conservatives, an' they want to make things better by makin' rich people richer an' poor people poorer.' It might still be funny, but it would at once acquire a shading of aggressive propagandist intention. As a character remarks in another, more recent and more radical children's book, Susan Price's *From Where I Stand*:

'Ah. It'll be something left-wing, then, if *he* calls them "political" in that voice-of-doom. The Tories aren't political, you know. They just are.'[12]

This is a very small instance, introduced simply for illustration's sake, of something which is present to some degree in all fiction and intrinsic to its nature. There is no act of self-censorship by which a writer can exclude or disguise the essential self. Sometimes, moreover, the conscious surface ideology and the passive ideology of a novel are at odds with each other, and 'official' ideas contradicted by unconscious assumptions. Since this is by no means true of fiction only, the skills of analysis applied to different levels of a text should form part of teacher training in any society which hopes for adequate literacy. By teaching children how to develop an alert enjoyment of stories, we are also equipping them to meet linguistic malpractices of more consequential kinds.

To associate the ideology of children's books with ideology in its broader definitions, we need to consider the third dimension of its presence. This is the one to which developments in literary theory, by now familiar and widely accepted, have introduced us, and the one from which domestic skirmishing between book people and child people has tended to distract our attention. In order to affirm its general nature, I take a convenient summary of its position from a study not of children's literature but of sixteenth-century poetry:

> How does ideology affect literary texts? The impact of ideology upon the writings of a particular society – or, for that matter, on the conventions and strategies by which *we* read those writings – is no different from the way it influences any other cultural practice. In no case, in Macherey's words, does the writer, as the producer of the text, manufacture the materials with which he works. The power of ideology is inscribed within the words, the rule-systems, and codes which constitute the text. Imagine ideology as a powerful force hovering over us as we read a text; as we read it reminds us of what is correct, commonsensical, or 'natural'. It tries, as it were, to guide both the writing and our subsequent readings of a text into coherence. When a text is written, ideology works to make some things more natural to write; when a text is read, it works to conceal struggles and repressions, to force language into conveying only those meanings reinforced by the dominant forces of our society.[13]

If this is true, as I believe it is, we must think in terms which include but also transcend the idea of individual authorship, and reappraise the relationship between the author and the reader. In the case of children's literature, our thinking may be affected by an over-simplified stereotype of possible authority and influence. The individual writer is likely, as we have seen, to make conscious choices about the explicit ideology of his work, while the uniqueness of imaginative achievements rests on the private, unrepeatable configurations which writers make at subconscious level from the common stock of their experience. Our habit is so much to cherish individualism, however, that we often overlook the huge commonalities of an age, and the captivity of mind we undergo by living in our own time and place and no other. A large part of any book is written not by its author but by the world its author lives in. To accept the point one has only to recognize the rarity of occasions when a writer manages to recolour the meaning of a single word: almost all the time we are the acquiescent prisoners of other people's meanings. As a rule, writers for children are transmitters not of themselves uniquely, but of the worlds they share.

For modern children's writing this has many implications, but I would pick out two. First, the writer's ability to reshape his world is strictly limited. It is in his power (and may be his duty) to recommend an improved world, reflecting not what it is but what he hopes it might be. But this undertaking is bound by the same constraint as the literature of warning, which depicts a corrupted world as the author *fears* it truly is or might be. The starting point for each must be a shared understanding of the present, and an actuality which the young reader believes in.

The second point is that we may live in a period when our common ideology has many local fractures, so that children in different parts of the same national society are caught between bonding and difference. If children who are citizens of one country live in worlds within a world, discrete subcultures within a culture, they will need different storytelling voices to speak to them – voices which can speak within an ideology which for them is coherent and complete. As I hope this discussion has indicated, ideology is inseparable from language, and divergences of language within a national culture point to divisions and fragmentations in its shared ideology. In Britain as in other countries there is indeed a common language, but when that is said it must be qualified. Britain is also a country of many languages, many Englishes, and the children who speak them ideally need both a common national literature and local literatures which speak to and for themselves. Robert Leeson makes this point in his case for 'alternative' publishing for children. He begins by

15

referring specifically to the spoken language and to dialect.

> The very richness of non-standard English is in itself a challenge to the whole system of education and literature, but a challenge that must be met. London schools at the moment are grappling (or not grappling) with new streams of language like Creole.[14]

He goes on to argue that 'alternative' publications need not be subject to the orthodox scrutiny of critics 'provided [they] can meet the critical response of [their] readers'. Interestingly he then goes on to make two significant conflations of ideas: first, he associates linguistic and literary subcultures with the literature of 'progressive' values, and second, he associates alternative publishing of books *for* children with publishing of books *by* children.

> So far the alternative publishers have not made great inroads into the field of fiction for the young. There have been some feminist stories for small children, some teenage writings, original and re-told folk stories from ethnic minorities. These are modest beginnings.[15]

The point which is half made here can be fully understood in its general implications if we define 'ideology' largely and precisely enough. The two points are crucial: subcultures of language are inseparable from the climate of ideas and values which are at work in them, and children inhabiting a subculture need to create a literature of their own, not merely be supplied with one. Leeson's ideas on this point are important and helpful but unnecessarily restricted in their scope. Like many other commentators, he is in practice most concerned with the London community of ethnic minorities and progressive groups. Such critics tend to write as if other places, other social groupings, other sites of active dialects, other schemes of ethical values did not exist, or had no comparable needs. If our thinking about ideology is clear enough, it is apparent that the same considerations apply to *all* children in any part of society (and in practice this probably means all parts of society) where there is tension between a common ideology and local circumstances. To appreciate the implications for children's literature demands acceptance that we do indeed inhabit a fragmented society, where each of the fragments needs and deserves to feel a confident sense of its value. As Leeson argues – but with a wider inference than he draws from it – we need a national children's literature (not to mention an international one) but also local literatures for particular racial or regional or social or (why not?) sexual groups, and also a literature made by the children themselves. Only when we have a coherent definition of ideology does this become adequately clear.

The reader as ideologist

Above all, it emerges from this argument that ideology is not something which is transferred to children as if they were empty receptacles. It is something which they already possess, having drawn it from a mass of experiences far more powerful than literature.

In literature, as in life, we have to start from where the children are, and with their own (often inarticulate) ideology. This offends some commentators, who prefer the literature to begin where they wish the children were, or assume that easy transformations can be made by humanely open-minded critical inquiry, whether based in classrooms or elsewhere. Rob Grunsell, describing his experiences in running an alternative school for chronic truants in London, reports the discomfiting consequences of moving too rationally and openly beyond a pre-existent teenage ideology:

> At lunch they had opinions in plenty, particularly about the blacks and the Pakis. It seemed to me such an obvious place to start, so I planned out a lesson on racial attitudes – a straight survey of what they thought, with no judgements and no 'right' answers. They designed the questionnaire with me, enjoying filling in their answers. From that point on it was a disaster. The answers weren't the same. 'Was Jimmy right?', why were they wrong? I couldn't convince them, because they couldn't listen, that there were no right answers. Here, in a lesson, hating Pakis because they're 'dim' and 'chicken' was obviously wrong. They sensed what I thought, even though I hadn't said it. They had lost, as usual, and more hopelessly than usual since they could do nothing about it. My prize-winning lesson in open-ended exploratory learning produced five miserable, depressed people.[16]

A similar result is produced by much over-confident surface didacticism in modern children's books, as it is by much persuasive rationality in classroom discussion. Where the ideology is explicit, it does not matter how morally unanswerable the substance is if it speaks persuasively only to those who are persuaded already, leaving others with their own divergent ideology intensified by resentful bemusement.

Susan Price's *From Where I Stand*, which I referred to earlier, is a passionately anti-racist story which operates very much at the level of conscious authorial intention. At one point a highly intelligent Bangladeshi teenager, Kamla, is interviewed by the headmistress of her comprehensive school about an anti-racist pamphlet she has helped to compose. The headmistress tries to reason with her:

'You are going to tell me that Asian and black children are often teased and bullied by white children in this school. This isn't news to me, you know. I am quite aware of it. Whenever I can, I intervene, I punish children who are caught bullying or robbing others – but I punish them for bullying, for blackmail, for theft, not for racism. You see, it isn't always wise to tackle these things head on, my dear; I wonder if you can understand that? These attitudes are entrenched. Unfortunately, many of the children here have parents who are racist in their views. In that case, if you attack the opinion, then you attack the parents, and you are telling the children that their parents are bad people – now, that doesn't help. It only antagonizes them, reinforces their beliefs . . . And they are only *children*, Kamla.'[17]

Susan Price's storytelling is very skilfully organized to discredit the headmistress by presenting her as one who is at best evasive and negligent in her efforts to subdue racist behaviour, and at worst has racist sympathies herself. The speech quoted above is thus placed in a context designed to undermine it. Readers are intended to conclude that the reasons for inaction given in the last sentences – reasons which are put forward often by real teachers in the real world – are merely disreputable rationalizations of unprincipled tolerance, if not something worse, with the implication that such reasons usually are. Susan Price is using literary skills to checkmate her opponents in an ideological chess game. But in the imperfect world these are genuine problems for teachers who try to educate children in anti-racist morality. It is unfortunately true that well-disposed ideological enthusiasm can be counter-productive in school classrooms; and it can be likewise in stories. So the likely effect of Susan Price's storytelling is to deepen children's entrenched attitudes, good and bad alike. If it were not so, the stresses on our social fabric would be a great deal easier to deal with.

Locating the ideology of individual books

I have argued, therefore, that we should accept both the omnipresence of ideology and the realities of fragmentation, divergence, passivity, inertia, conservatism, invisibility, unreasoningness, in much of its expression and reception by the author and the child. Although it is easiest to illustrate the ideological process from the repertoire of *active* ideology in progressive modern fiction, that is only because didactic content is more obtrusive there, not because it is present on a larger scale than it is in traditional fiction. On all sides, in numerous commentaries on children's fiction (not to mention many novels themselves) a customary error is to make the wrong implicit analogy, by treating ideology as if it were a political policy, when in fact it is a climate of belief. The first can be changed, and itemized, and imposed, and legislated into reality and (though not always!) vindicated by pure reason. The second is vague, and holistic, and pliant, and stable, and can only evolve.

The first priority is to understand how the ideology of any given book can be located. Above all, such an understanding is important for teachers, especially primary school teachers and English specialists. Their task is to teach children how to read, so that to the limits of each child's capacity that child will not be at the mercy of *what* she reads. I shall conclude, then, with some examples of the kind of question which teachers in training might usefully be taught to ask about children's books, in order to clarify the ideology which is working in them. They are mostly questions which adults generally might find interesting in order to test their own recreational fiction, and which can easily be modified for use in classrooms. The purpose, as I have tried to indicate throughout, is a modest one: not to evaluate, discredit or applaud a writer's ideology, but simply to see what it is.

The questions are only examples, and teachers and others will readily be able to augment them.

1. What happens if the components of a text are transposed or reversed (as I suggested might be done with Richmal Crompton's political joke in *William the Bad*)? Does examination of the negative, so to speak, show unsuspected blights in the published picture? In particular, do we observe that a book which seems to be asserting a principle is only attacking a symptom? Is this 'anti-sexist novel' in fact sexist itself, and merely anti-male? Does this war story attack the Germans for atrocities which are approved when the British inflict them?

2. Consider the dénouements of some books, and the happy (or unhappy) ending. Does the happy ending of a novel amount to a 'contract of reaffirmation' of questionable values which have earlier

seemed to be on trial? Is the conclusion imaginatively coherent, or does it depend on implicit assumptions which are at odds with the surface ideology? Are there any loose ends (not so much of plot but of thought and feeling)? (Although it is not a children's book, students may find a particularly interesting example in the closing paragraphs of Richard Hughes's *A High Wind in Jamaica*.) If some 'happy endings' reconverge on the dominant ideology, is it also true that an unhappy ending is a device for denying such reconvergence, and hence for reinforcing a blend of ideological and emotional protest? (Students might consider the brilliantly effective unhappy endings of Susan Price's *Twopence a Tub* and Jan Mark's *Divide and Rule*.)

3. Are the values of a novel shown as a 'package' in which separate items appear to interlock? For example, does one story condemn racial prejudice and social class prejudice as if they were automatically interdependent, and does another in the same way celebrate a seemingly inseparable threesome made up of patriotism, courage and personal loyalty? (*Biggles* books are a good source of study on 'packaging' of various kinds.) Are these groups of virtues or vices necessarily or logically connected with each other? Are they being grouped together in order to articulate some larger, aggregated virtue or vice, such as 'white Britishness'? Students may find it interesting to bring this exercise to bear comparatively on the work of W.E. Johns and some current socially progressive fiction. Is it in fact a mark of quality in a book that it differentiates its values rather than fusing them in composite and (perhaps frauduently) homogeneous groups?

4. Is it a noticeable feature of some major 'classic' children's books that they test and undermine some of the values which they superficially appear to be celebrating? (I think it is. Students may find it interesting to perform this experimental inquiry on *Treasure Island*, *The Wind in the Willows*, and *Stalky and Co*, as well as *Tom Sawyer* and *Huckleberry Finn*.) Are there any modern children's books which seem to work in similar ways? Readers may find, for example, that the novels of John Christopher (notably *Fireball*) and Peter Dickinson (notably *Healer*) are more complex than they seem.

There is an important general point here. As recent studies based in modern critical theory have convincingly shown, many major works will sustain more radical and subversive readings than we are accustomed to. Critiques of children's literature which concentrate on surface ideology tend to ignore such possibilities. They observe only the external conservative values detectable in some major children's books, and overlook the radical questioning to which the text exposes them. The fallacy (as I have earlier suggested in the case of *Huckleberry Finn*) often lies in treating the novel as if it were some other kind of writing, and so ignoring narrative procedures which are basic to its meanings. If critics can make such mistakes, so can children: they need our help in learning how to read. But that is no excuse for suppressing or reclassifying the books.

5. Are desirable values associated with niceness of character, and vice versa? Is it really true that a given attractive philosophy or action could not believably be held or performed by someone whose character was in other ways unpleasant? How much allowance is there (and how much should there be in a children's book) for inconsistency, or for dissonance between ideology and temperament? How far is a book's ideology conveyed by 'moral symmetry' in character delineation?

6. Does anyone in a story have to make a difficult *choice* – of behaviour, loyalties, values, etc. – in which there is more than one defensible course of action? Or does the plot hinge merely on a predetermined choice, and interest depend on whether or not it is successfully carried out?

7. Is any character shown as performing a mixture of roles, especially roles with sharply differentiated contexts of friendship, safety or prestige? Does any character belong as an accepted member in more than one subculture or group, and move without stress between them? If any character does so, is one such group presented by the author as deserving higher value than another? The groups may be as simple as school (both staff and peer group) and family. They may, on the other hand, extend to differences of race, culture, religion, political affiliation and social custom, as they do for example in *Kim*. *Kim* is an excellent text for students to consider, because it exposes the need for caution in using the vocabulary of political judgement, in this case 'racist', as a generalizing critical terminology.

8. Last and most important in this selection is the question of omission and invisibility. Who are the people who 'do not exist' in a given story? This may mean people who are present but humanly downgraded, as if inscribed above the writer's desk were the words 'All human beings are human, but some are more human than others.' Downgraded groups include servants, but may also in a given case include teachers, or even parents. More seriously, they may include criminals and policemen. More seriously still, they may include foreigners, soldiers, girls, women and blacks. These last groups are more serious invisibilities because they do not plausibly represent mere story conventions, but curtailments of humanity embedded in an ideology.

Omission takes many forms: for example, the performance of important life-supporting tasks for children without any reference to the workers (such as mothers) who carry them out. Invisibility may take many forms, for example, the denial of names, the identification of people by what they do rather than what they are, and the absorption of individuals into social and racial groups. It can be helpful again to take an 'adult' text before considering children's books with students, and the most rewarding one I know to introduce this inquiry is Conrad's *Heart of Darkness*.

Taken together, questions such as these may serve effectively to lift ideology 'off the page' and bring it from obscure and unexpected places into the light, but it need not and should not suppress the uniqueness of individual stories, or convert them into cadavers for pedagogic dissection or for classroom autopsy. What we call 'ideology', as I have tried to argue, is a living thing, and something we need to know as we need to know ourselves. Very much like that, because it is a part of us.

REFERENCES

1. C.S. Lewis, 'On Three Ways of Writing for Children', reprinted in *Only Connect* edited by Sheila Egoff et al, Oxford University Press, Canada, 1980, page 208.
2. Robert Leeson, *Reading and Righting*, Collins, 1985, page 161.
3. Fred Inglis, *The Promise of Happiness*, Cambridge University Press, 1981, page 7.
4. Bob Dixon, *Catching Them Young 1, Sex, Race and Class in Children's Fiction*, Pluto Press, 1977, page 95.
5. Leeson, pages 169-170.
6. Nina Bawden, 'The Imprisoned Child', in *The Thorny Paradise* edited by Edward Blishen, Kestrel, 1975, pages 63-4.
7. Lewis, page 120.
8. Henry Treece, 'Writing for Children', in Owens and Marland (eds.), *The Practice of English Teaching*, Blackie, 1970, page 176.
9. Mark Twain, *Huckleberry Finn*, chapter 32.
10. P.W. Musgrave, *From Brown to Bunter: The Life and Death of the School Story*, Routledge & Kegan Paul, 1985, page 17.
11. Richmal Crompton, *William the Bad*, Newnes, 1930, Chapter 3.
12. Susan Price, *From Where I Stand*, Faber & Faber, 1984, page 60.
13. Gary Waller, *English Poetry of the Sixteenth Century*, Longman, 1986, page 10.
14. Leeson, page 179.
15. Leeson, page 180.
16. Rob Grunsell, *Born to be Invisible*, Macmillan Education, 1978, page 50.
17. Price, page 119.